Alexan

THE TWELVE
and
THE SCYTHIANS

translated and introduced
by Jack Lindsay

with an afterword
by Yuri Molok

illustrated
by Yuri Annenkov

The Journeyman Press
London & West Nyack

First Russian edition published in Moscow, 1918
This translation published by the Journeyman Press, 1982
97 Ferme Park Road, Crouch End, London N8 9SA and
17 Old Mill Road, West Nyack, NY 10994

Journeyman *Chapbook* 8

ISBN 0 904526 49 6

The Journeyman Press gratefully acknowledges the financial
assistance of the Arts Council of Great Britain in the production
of this volume of the *Chapbook* series.

The Journeyman *Chapbook* series

1. *The Ballad of Reading Gaol* by Oscar Wilde, illustrated by Frans
Masereel
2. *The Overcoat* by Nicolai Gogol, translated by David Magarshack
and decorated by John Edward Craig
3. *Shelley's Socialism* by Edward Aveling and Eleanor Marx Aveling,
and *Popular Songs* by Percy Bysshe Shelley
4. *The Radical Imagination: Frans Masereel* by Josef Herman
5. *The Story of the Irish Citizen Army* by Sean O'Casey
6. *The Novel on Blue Paper* by William Morris, edited and introduced
by Penelope Fitzgerald
7. *The City of the Sun* by Thomas Campanella, translated by A.M.
Elliott and R. Millner, and introduced by A.L. Morton
8. *The Twelve, and the Scythians* by Alexander Blok, illustrated by
Yuri Annenkov, translated and introduced by Jack Lindsay, with an
afterword by Yuri Molok

Printed in Great Britain

ALEXANDER BLOK AND THE SYMBOLISTS

by Jack Lindsay

Russian symbolist poetry, of which Blok was the greatest exponent, was started off by Valeri Bryusov (1873-1924), member of a rich Moscow merchant family, who in 1894-5 published at his own cost three booklets, *Russian Symbolism*, which included translations or imitations of the most advanced Western poets. He was deeply moved by the work of Baudelaire, Mallarmé, Rimbaud, Verlaine, Maeterlinck, Verhaeren. He thus introduced suddenly into Russian poetry the poets who most powerfully struggled to grasp and define the alienating or dehumanising forces of European industrial society. The effect was shattering. In 1899 was founded the publishing house 'Scipio', and Bryusov, drawn on to its board, became in effect its director. By 1904 he organised the periodical *Vesy* (The Balance) devoted to symbolist work. Conscripted in 1914, he cooperated with the Bolsheviks in 1917, joined the Communist Party in 1919, and worked at various projects of the Department of Education, founding the Historical Institute in Moscow in 1921. Though the symbolist school had more or less broken down about 1912, it had done its fructifying work. Its ideas and methods strongly influenced the younger poets such as Mayakovsky, Klebnikov, Burlyuk.

An important symbolist was Andrei Bely (Andrew the White), whose real name was Bugayev. Born in 1880, he lived till 1934. He worked on the board of *Vesy* and was much affected by the mystic and poet, Solovyev, son of an important historian, who merged ideas of the Slavophiles, Hegel, Schopenhauer and Hartmann, the Ukrainian mystic Skovoroda, Plato and eastern mysticism, dominated by the idea of Sophia, the heavenly Wisdom (seen also as the Eternal Feminine Spirit, the Muse). Bely's work strongly affected such young poets as Blok, Pasternak, Aseyev. The world was felt to exist as the shadow of a reality which was grasped by poets in their moments of creative exaltation. In 1913-6, after some periods abroad, Bely joined the literary group, the 'Scythians', and hailed the revolution. After 1918 he worked in various cultural organisations.

The symbolists then merged a deep sense of the environing world of the bourgeoisie as alienating people from reality, from themselves, their fellows, and nature, with a passionate quest for the forces capable of breaking through the impasse. They were always on the lookout for movements coming up from below in the people and threatening the corrupted world with cataclysm, with breakthrough on to new levels of human integration and freedom. These attitudes gave them their distinctive Russian qualities which they handed on in various forms to the younger poets coming up.

Blok (1880-1921) had as father a professor of law at Warsaw University and as mother the daughter of a botanist rector at St Petersburg University, who herself wrote poetry. The marriage broke down and he was brought up by his mother, to whom he was devoted. In 1903 he married the actress Lyubov, daughter of the chemist Mendeleyev, and published his first poems. The Soloyevian symbols first cohered for him in the image of the Beautiful Lady (1904), expressing creative and sexual energy, but capable of turning into a mere carnal lure. Blok throughout was concerned with inner and outer conflict, with the potentialities of transformation into higher or lower forms. In December 1901 he wrote, 'I have split into two . . . for I involved doubles.' Among his opposed images were those of Pierrot and Harlequin, Monk and Knight Errant. As late as December 1920 he wrote to his wife:

> It is quite true that there is much I wish to 'disintegrate' and that I have my 'doubts', but that is not 'art' for art's sake, but stems from an extremely exacting attitude towards life; from the fact that I think that what cannot be 'disintegrated' will not disintegrate but will merely be purified. I do not consider myself in the least a pessimist.

The struggle in art as in life, he says, if truly and whole-heartedly carried on, cannot but result in the emergence of what is more fully human, integrated on a new level. His poetry is at all phases haunted by symbolic figures who one way or another sum up the most vital or dynamic forces at work in people, the forces of history moulding them and driving them on — forces that are the people themselves in their deepest and fullest aspects. The Beautiful Lady, the Stranger, Russia, Christ were for him the symbols of these forces at work in himself and in his people. The strongly personal element inhibited a coherent system, but at the same time provided a ceaseless dynamic of growth and reapplication of the symbols within his poetic system. A strong movement on to the historical level came with the poem, *On Kulikovo Battlefield*, with its apocalyptic elements.

Called up in 1916, Blok served in a sanitary division behind the lines in the Pinsky Marshes. But soon after the February Revolution in 1917 he was back in the capital. His diary enables us to follow his reactions to the situation in all their complexity and depth of feeling. He was worried that 'intelligence, morals and above all art' were becoming 'an object of hate'. 'This is one of the most terrible flames of the revolutionary conflagration', for 'such is the psychology of all "senseless" perturbations' (using Pushkin's term). But his sympathies were with the workers. He was alarmed at the emergence of a new reaction even before July. 'All over the city cadet shock troops, imperialists, bourgeois and stock brokers are lifting their heads . . . Twilight. Could it be? Again — into the night, into horror, into despair.' A week before the October (7 November) uprising he wrote: 'Yesterday a major split among the Bolsheviks occurred at the Soviet of

Workers' and Soldiers' Deputies. Zinoviev, Trotsky and others considered an uprising on the 20th to be necessary, whatever its outcome, which they viewed pessimistically. *Only Lenin believes that the capture of power by democracy will really end the war and set everything right in the country.*' (The italics are his. Bryusov had also been stressing Lenin's role.) On 7 August Blok wrote:

> *The task of Russian culture* is to direct . . . fire on that which must be burned; to transform the violence of Stenka and Yemelka [peasant leaders of revolts in the 17th and 18th centuries] into a purposeful musical wave; to set up such barriers to destruction which, without reducing the pressure of the fire, would on the contrary organise the pressure; to organise the elemental forces.

On 3 December he began writing his essay, *The Intelligentsia and the Revolution.* On 3 January the poet Esenin called and spent the evening with him. They had a long discussion. Blok raised the question of the people's attitude to the intelligentsia. Esenin declared that the intellectual 'is like a bird in a cage; the huge, sinewy hand (of the people) reaches out to him; he flutters and cries in terror. But he will be taken . . . And let free (an upsweeping gesture).' On 8 January Blok began *The Twelve.* 'All day — "The Twelve". An inward trembling.'

His essay is closely linked throughout with the ideas and emotions concentrated in the poem. He makes first a rapid review of the past decade, the review of a man who has experienced the years 1906-1916, 'a few years which weigh down on the shoulders like a long, sleepless night filled with phantoms', simultaneously a personal and social drama. 'I think I was not the only one to experience the feeling of morbidity and depression.' Then came the heartening storm of October. The stifling atmosphere of reaction, the world-war which proved to be 'the fitting crown of the falsehood, filth, and loathsomeness in which our country was steeped,' then at last the 'stream' of the revolution which 'began in the "bloodless idyll" of the February days and was expanding ceaselessly and menacingly,' changing 'the whole European atmosphere.'

'We Russians,' he writes, 'are living through an epoch which has few its equal in grandeur.' He recalls Tyutchev's words: 'Blessed is he who has visited the world in its fateful moments,' and takes up Gogol's image of Russia as a galloping troika. 'It is not the artist's task to watch the implementation of plans, to worry over whether they will materialise or not . . . it is the artist's task, the artist's *duty* to see the plans, to hear the music "blaring in the windtorn air".' He reports what he had written in 1916: 'Life is worth living only to place boundless demands on it: all or nothing.' What is now planned?

> *To change everything.* To make it so that everything turns new; that our deceitful, filthy, dull, ugly life might turn into a just, pure, merry and beautiful one. When *such* intentions, forever lurking in the human soul, the soul of the people, tear the chains shackling them and break forth in a turbulent stream,

shattering dams and washing away superfluous chunks of shores — this is
called revolution. Anything lesser, more moderate, more lowly is called a
rebellion, a riot . . . But this is called a *revolution*.

Its shattering force is akin to the fiercest phenomena of nature.

Woe betide those who expect to find in revolution the fulfilment of only their
own dreams, however lofty and noble they may be. Revolution, like a
whirlwind, like a snowstorm, always carries something new and unexpected; it
cruelly disappoints many; it often washes the unworthy to dry land unscathed.
But these are details that do not affect the general course of the stream, nor the
menacing, deafening roar it emits. In any case the roar is always about
something *great*.

Peace and friendship of nations, this is the sign under which the Russian
revolution unfurls. This is what the stream roars about. This is the music which
he who has ears should hear.

We see then why the action of *The Twelve* is set in a violent snowstorm.
'Bolshevism — the elements,' he noted down more than once. The term music
he uses to define the full sweep of purpose, which goes beyond the ideas or hopes
of any single participant: a sweep which includes the processes of nature as well
as human process, individual or social. It expresses the full dialectic of the
situation. (In 1929 Bely wrote an essay on 'Rhythm as Dialectics'.)

On 28 January 1918 Blok completed the poem. 'Today I am a genius.' *The
Scythians* was written during the next two days. *The Twelve* had depicted the
people breaking violently through the limits of the old world and bringing about
a new dispensation, new level of human unity and brotherhood (Christ), despite
the inevitably constricted vision of each individual taking part in the transformation. In *The Scythians* Blok then turned to the relation of this new world to the
rest of Europe, where no revolutionary changes were visible. A new
contradiction had been brought into existence. Would it be possible for the other
lands to recognise what had happened, and to move in their own ways on to the
new level? If they failed to understand, new terrible stresses and conflicts could
not but emerge.

The Twelve had an immediate and vast effect. Phrases from it were endlessly
repeated; hoardings and banners all over Russia bore extracts. The closeness
with which Blok was eagerly following the course of events as he wrote the poem
is shown by the way it now and then echoes headlines from *Pravda*, e.g. the issue
of 3 January which stresses the need to warn the workers against the supporters
of the Constituent Assembly. 'Be on your guard, Hold your rifle firm.' The call
to keep one's eyes peeled echoes a poem by Demian Bednyi in *Pravda*, 5
January. Bednyi recognised the link: 'What a good pupil of mine has appeared.'

All the elements that had gone to build Blok's symbolism appear in *The
Twelve*, but unified with a new intensity. From one angle we could call it a

Harlequinade. Katya is the Beautiful Lady in her most carnal aspects; she is also Christ, betrayed and killed by Judas-Vanka; she is also fat-rumped Russia. But to attempt to analyse the poem back into such earlier elements is to lose the new depth of poetic consciousness in which at last symbols and life, history and the individual, have become indissolubly one.

Blok wrote a small amount of verse after January 1918, but it adds little to his achievement. Not that he was idle. He wrote such things as the play *Ramzes* (Rameses), which Gorky commissioned and which uses ancient Egypt as a simplified setting for the problems of labour and the struggles of the workers. He had been among the intellectuals who at Smolny declared their readiness to work with the Soviets. In January 1918 he began work on a commission for publishing literary classics; he served in the Repertoire Section of the Petrograd Theatre Department of the People's Commissariat for Education; at Gorky's invitation he worked also for the publishers, *World Literature*; in 1919 he was chairman of the Board of the Bolshoi Drama Theatre, and in 1920 chairman of the Petrograd section of the All-Russian Poets' Union. Three months before his death he was welcomed with great enthusiasm at a Personal Evening in the Leningrad Theatre of Drama. He died on 7 August 1921.

How strongly he has continued to be felt as a key-figure in the creation of a new culture may be seen from a poem written by Voznesensky in 1964, in which occurs the moral: 'All progress is retrogression, if the process breaks people down':

> Russia my land, home of Beauty,
> land of Rublev, Blok and Lenin,
> where the snow falls enthralling
> as pure and white as purest linen:
> she has no higher calling
> than to bring
>   the world
>   to salvation.

THE TWELVE

[1]

Black night.
White snow.
Wind O wind!
It knocks you down as you go.
Wind O wind —
Through God's world blowing.

The wind whirls
The flurrying snow.
Ice slides up from below.
Tricky and sly,
The going's dead slow.
You'll slip if you hurry.

From house to house, see
A cord has been slung.
A sign on it's hung:
'All Power to the Constituent Assembly!'
An old woman weeps at the sight,
Can't make out the things they write,
What's that big poster doing up there?
How many footrags could be
Cut from its cloth, yet our kids all go bare,
No shoes, only tatters to wear.

Like a hen she fumbles, stumbles,
On the top of a snowdrift, and mumbles,
'Holy Mother, pray for us, pray.
Those Reds will be the death of me.'

The wind strikes deep as it blows.
There's a sting in the frost.
At the crossroads the bourgeois, lost,
Pulls his collar up over his nose.

Who's that chap with the long hair,
Muttering with downcast air:
'Everywhere treason,
Russia sunk in the mire.'
A writer: is that the reason
For such talk? A speechifier.

And you, skulking by the drift,
Long-skirted, a scowl on your brow,
What is it worries you now,
Comrade priest?

Recall how you strutted, well-pleased,
With your belly stuck out, and a cross
Hanging heavily there,
Among the poor folk?

A fine lady in astrakhan cloak
Chats with a friend, 'O my dear,
How we cried and cried, my heart broke.'
Down she trips, slips
Flat on her face.

Hey, come here,
Heave her up, hey!

The frisky wind flirts,
Tossing up skirts,
Maliciously gay,
Swinging legs this and that way,
Rips, tears up, and scatters
The magnificent sign:
'All Power to the Constituent Assembly!'
Denounces and chatters:

Our own Assembly we called . . .
In this house we all met at last . . .
Our debate we held . . .
This resolution we passed:
Ten for a short time, twentyfive the whole night.
No undercutting, it isn't right . . .
Come quick to bed.

The night's late.
Not a soul in the street.
A lone lost tramp
Shuffles, stoops low.
Winds whine and hiss.

Hey, you poor dear
Come over here.
Give us a kiss.

Bread.
What's that ahead?
Hurry, I say.

Black, black skies.

Rage, seething rage,
Nothing assuages it,
Black rage, holy rage.

Comrade, keep your eyes
Skinned in this wind.

[2]

Wind twirls merrily, snowflakes dance.
Through the night twelve men advance.

Slings on the black rifles they bear.
Lights here and there, lights everywhere.

Chewing fags, caps pulled askew.
Convict clothes the best would do.

Freedom, freedom,
Hey ho, with no cross.
Tra-ta-ta.

It's freezing, comrades. What a frost.

Vanka and Katya to the pub have rushed.
Kerensky-banknotes in her stockings she pushed.

Vanka's got rich, no matter how.
Hitched up with them, ditched us now.

Vanka, son of a bitch, get away.
Keep your bourgeois hands off Katya, I say.

Freedom, freedom,
Hey ho, with no cross
Vanka's busy with that Kate.
What do you think he's busy at?

Tra-ta-ta.

Lights here and there, lights everywhere.
The rifle slings are caught in the glare.

Revolution-time we all must keep.
The enemy's relentless, doesn't sleep.

Comrade, throw out all fear. Why not?
Into Holy Russia let's fire a shot —

Rough-and-tumble dump,
Wood huts in a clump,
And a big fat rump.

Hey ho, with no cross.

[3]

To do their bit our lads stood fast
To join up with the Red Guards O
To join up with the Red Guards O
And lay their wild heads down at last

Ah, life is bitter.
Life is a lot of fun.
Old greatcoat in tatters
And Austrian gun.

Beware, you bourgeoisie, beware.
We're going to set the world aflame,
Blood and blazes everywhere,
Lord, bless our game!

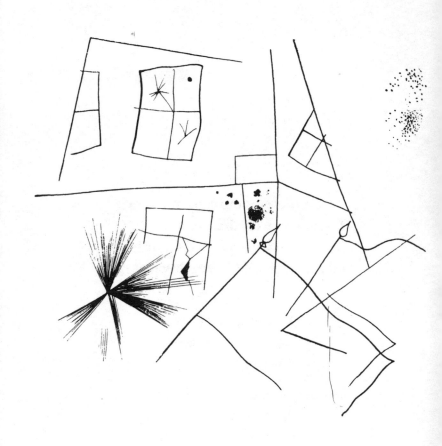

[4]

The cabby bawls, the bright snow whirls,
Katya and Vanka go hurtling gay.
Electric beams are streaming
Along the shafts —
Out of the way!

An army greatcoat on his back,
His face as silly as face can be,
He twists high his moustache of black,
Plays about and twiddles it,
Trying out his wit.

There goes Vanka, thickset shoulders,

There goes Vanka, talks and shouts,
That fool of a Katya in his arms
Can't resist such charms.

See her tilt her head back, bolder,
Her teeth gleam pearly with her laughter,

O my Katya, Katya dear,
Katya with your chubby snout.

[5]

Across your throat, my carefree Katya,
There are scratches bleeding red.
There's a pouting hole that's bled
Underneath your left breast, Katya.

Hey ho, dance away,
Give a firstclass leg-display.

Your gawdy drawers were trimmed with lace,
Trot ahead now, trot ahead.
Officers were yours to embrace.
Get to bed then, get to bed.

Hey ho, fall into bed.
Make my pulses madly race.

That captain of yours, have you forgotten?
When he grabbed you, you'd almost swoon.
I knifed him, yes, he's dead and rotten.
Don't tell me you forget so soon.

Hey ho, give me a thrill.
Into your bed invite me still.

You flaunted those fine gaiters of grey
And nibbled bonbons, the expensive kind.
With cadets you used to play.
Now privates are all that you can find.

Hey ho, sin your best.
Rock those worries of yours to rest.

ю. А.

[6]

Again the cabby gallops along
Fullspeed, and roars a rowdy song.

Halt, Andrukha. Help me here.
Petrukha, run round to the rear.

Rat tatarat tat tat tat tat.
The snow spirts up, then again is flat.

Look, the cabby and Vanka run.
Get it right now. Cock the gun.

Rat taratat. You should have known.
· · · · · · · · ·
Leave another fellow's piece alone.

Ho, the skunk, he got away.
Tomorrow I will make you pay.

But where is Katya? Katya's dead.
A bullet through her head

Happy now, Katya? I'd like to know.
Sprawl there, carrion, in the snow.

Revolution-time we all must keep.
The relentless enemy doesn't sleep.

[7]

The twelve again are advancing further.
Rifles firm on shoulders they place.
Only the wretch who did the murder
Doesn't dare to show his face.

Faster he goes in the wintry weather.
Round his neck a scarf he twists and ties.
See, he can't pull himself together,
Can't get his bearings however he tries.

Why so downcast, comrade, why?
Why so cheesed-off? Tell me straight.
A hangdog look is in your eye.
You're not troubled about Kate?

Listen and I'll tell you, mates.
She was my girl, redhot stuff.
All those tipsy summer nights,
I never had enough.

What got me was the eyes she had,
Just like cat's eyes in the dark.
On her right shoulderblade the birthmark
showed in a soft smudge of red.
So I killed her and she's dead.
Damn her, she drove me mad.

Now, Piotr, stow your snivel.
Like an old woman you drivel.
You've gone all to pieces.
Stop this maundering, please.
Take a grip on yourself, you.
We've better things to do.

Do you think these times are proper
For us to pat your head and nurse you?
All of us will come a cropper.
Things will soon be getting worse.

Petruka slows his shambling pace,
No longer he wants to run away,

Lifts his head, with clearing face,
His eyes once more are wildly gay.

Hey ho,
A bit of fun's no sin, I know.

Lock your rooms. Don't delay.
Looters are heading this way.

But open your cellars wide.
The down-and-outs won't be denied.

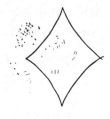

[8]

O blues, O boring blues,
    You deadly boring
        Boredom.

What time I've got
I'll spend, spend the lot.

On my head's a patch
That I'll scratch, scratch.

Sunflower seeds I don't lack,
I'll crack them, crack.

With my little knife,
I'll rip your life, rip.

Sparrow-quick, bourgeois, fly!
Your blood I'll drink as a toast
To the girl with dark brows I love most.
I love her, I don't deny.

Give rest O Lord to your handmaiden's soul.

What a bore.

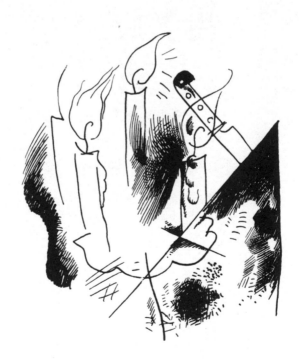

[9]

On Neva's tower a quiet falls.
The city's uproar now we lose.
No policeman in the streets at all.
We'll have a spree, though we've no booze.

The bourgeois at the crossroads stands
And round his nose he tucks the fur.
Tail between legs, beside him stinking
Skulks a mangy scruffy cur.

A questionmark, the bourgeois stands,
Silent and hungry, mongrel-like.
Behind him the old world is sinking,
Tail between legs, a mangy tyke.

[10]

The blizzard rages at its fiercest —
Blizzard ho, blizzard, hey!
You can't make out the chap that's nearest,
Only four odd paces away.

Funnels of snow rise whirling by,
Pillars of snow hold up the sky.

Saviour, there's a snowstorm raving.
Petka, what does your babble mean?
You had your Lord on the painted screen.
From what then were you ever saved?

You're not a brainy chap, we've seen.
Understand now, get it straight.
Your hands aren't clean.
They're bloody through the love of Kate.

Revolution-time we all must keep.
The relentless enemy doesn't sleep.
Forward forward forward then
You working-men.

[11]

The twelve keep on advancing there.
The holy name they've mocked.
No pity left to spare,
All things they're prepared to dare.

Their rifles are ready cocked,
Aimed at the unseen foe.
Through backlanes deeply blocked,
Nothing anywhere but snow.
Treacherous drifts. Take care.
One step and in you go.

Look well round.
The red flag's ahead.

Hark now, the sound
Of a measured tread.

The vicious foe
Is awake, beware.

The blizzard blurs their sight
Day and night
With no respite.

Forward forward forward then
you working-men!

[12]

On they march with victorious beat.
  Who's lurking there? Come out!
  Only the wind ahead they meet,
    Tossing the red flag about.

The snow piles up and bars the way.
  Who's in that drift? Come out.
  Nothing except a limping stray,
    dragging his hungry snout.

You scabby lout, I'll make you stir.
This bayonet will tickle you.
The old world is a mangy cur.
Off, or I'll stick you through.

Snarling wolf with droopy tail,
Teeth impotently bare,
Mongrel, the cold wind's a flail.
Answer. Who goes there?

Who waves a red flag through the din?
Damn the dark. I'm blind.
Who skulks behind the houses there?
Skurrying to save his skin.

Give in. Maybe your lives we'll spare.
We'll get you all the same.
Come out or a worse fate you'll find.
Come out, we're taking aim.

Rat-ta-tat. From all the houses
Come echoes, but no words we know.
Only the blizzard whoops, carouses,
In helpless merriment, on the snow.

Rat-ta-tat
Rat-ta-tat

So on they march with victorious tread.
The starveling cur trots in the rear.
Bearing the flag tempestuous red,
While blizzard blinds the world below,
Untouched by bullets whistling near,
Stepping across the storms of snow,
As snow-veils twist and veer
In white rose-gardens brightly iced
Leading the way is Jesus Christ.

THE SCYTHIANS

Panmongolism! Though the name is fierce
Yet it caresses my ear.

Vladimir Solovyov

You are millions. But we sweep an endless flood.
You'd stem our torrents? Ah, be wise.
For we are Scythians. Asia is our blood
And crowding hungers slant our eyes.

For you, slow centuries. For us, an hour.
Like slaves, subservient and abhorred,
We barred, a sprawled and mountainous power,
Your Europe from the Mongol Horde.

For centuries your hammering forges blurred
The crackling avalanche poised to fall.
And like a strange impossible tale you heard
Lisbon and then Messina call.

For centuries eastward all your dreams were bound,
You filched our pearls and hid the loot.
Mocking, you closed us in with guns around
And waited for the sign to shoot.

That time has come and doom has spread her wings.
Your insults thicken and we frown.
The hour will chime. We'll strike in angry rings
Your proud and impotent Paestums down.

Then pause, Old World, or soon your last hope sinks.
Wise, weary, worn, the portent lies.
Old Oedipus, you stand and face the Sphinx.
Spell the dark riddle of her eyes.

Russia the Sphinx. Exultant, suffering yet
And sweating blood, she seeks her fate.
Westward her eyes with lids of stone are set;
She holds you with her love, her hate.

The depths of love you exhausted long ago,
The love that racks us with its joys.
You've long forgotten the fierce love we know,
That burns and burningly destroys.

All things we love. Cold numbers' fever-fit
And visions marvellously caught.
All things we know: the luminous Gallic wit,
The German dusk's new worlds of thought.

All we remember, all. Montmartre's *Hell*,
Venetian breezes freshly blown,
The scents where far-off orange-blossoms swell,
Cologne's upheaving mass of stone.

And flesh we love, its taste, its tints and tones,
Its raw and mortal smell that draws.
Are we to blame then if one day your bones
Crack in our heavy gentle paws?

We catch the wildest colts, so great our strength.
They plunge, they vainly leap and shake.
Their restive jaws receive our bits at length
And women-slaves we tame or break.

Then leave your blackening ways of war, accept
Our clasp of peace before too late.
Sheathe the old sword and let the truce be kept,
Let brotherhood bring an end of hate.

If not, we know the trick of treacheries,
and things for us will be no worse.
But westward still for ruined centuries
Your children, weak and lost, will curse.

Your gloss-faced Europe through the unending plain
We'll lure within our forest-spaces,
Our tangled deeps, and turn on you again,
Swooping, our Asiatic faces.

Come to the Urals then, they're clear and wide,
And rage along the dark ravines.
With callous Science let the Horde collide,
The Mongols with the massed Machines.

No longer shall we then uphold the shield
Against your unprotected side.
We'll note the bloody and tumultuous field,
Unimplicated, slanting-eyed.

The ruthless Huns will strip our heaping dead,
They'll leave your cities charred and bare.
They'll stable horses in the churches, spread
Burnt smells of white flesh everywhere.

Old World, to work and peace where all is good,
We call, to happy days and nights.
For the last time to joyous brotherhood
The barbarian lute invites.

(January 1918. *Hell, L'Enfer,*
is the name of a tavern)

71

THE FIRST ILLUSTRATED EDITION OF 'THE TWELVE'

(Blok-Annenkov-Alconost)

by Yuri Molok

The interest which we feel for first editions, published during a writer's lifetime, inevitably extends to the writers' contemporaries, the artists who had occasion to be their first illustrators.

There are several examples of this in Russian culture. Lev Tolstoy's novel *Anna Karenina* first appeared in a journal accompanied by Leonid Pasternak's drawings. Here the artist's work was almost synchronous with that of the writer. This was also the case with Mayakovsky, who preferred Rodchenko or El Lissitsky as kindred 'poets of the new typography'.

Between these examples lies Alexander Blok's 'The Twelve' with drawings by Yuri Annenkov, the first illustrated edition of the poem, published by Alconost Press in Petrograd at the end of 1918.

Here we have a rare case. The testimonies of all three participants in this edition — poet, publisher and artist — have survived, and they permit us to attempt to briefly reconstruct the history of this unique book.

I

It cannot be said that Blok's poetry before 'The Twelve' had been ignored by artists. The foremost Russian graphic artists of the early twentieth century illustrated his verse and designed his books. The famous stage designer Bakst executed the frontispiece for the cycle of poems 'The Snow Mask'; Somov, author of the famous portrait of Blok, designed his book *The Theatre*; and Roerich provided a drawing for his 'Italian Poems', the original of which, presented to the poet by the artist, hung in Blok's study.

Nor was Blok himself indifferent to the publication of his books. He chose the typeface and typographical ornament and was well acquainted with all the fine points of book production. The publisher Samuil Alyansky of Alconost Press, set up in 1918, who actually published 'The Twelve', recalls that in his book enterprises he frequently followed the poet's advice.

But never before had Blok been so closely involved in the illustration of his work as in the case of 'The Twelve'.

The poem was received by his contemporaries as an epos of the revolution. It stepped beyond the bounds of literature and became the folklore of the revolutionary street. First printed on 3 March 1918 in the newspaper *Znamya truda* (Banner of Labour), it was posted up in the streets of Petrograd. The poem was recited on the stage, and lines from it formed the text of posters pasted up all over the city during revolutionary festivities. This was a revolution of the printed word, which the Constructivist El Lissitsky later describes as follows: 'The traditional book was torn up into separate lines, magnified a hundred times, painted more colourfully and hung up as a poster in the street.'

All these seemingly non-bookish forms of the poem's existence suggested the idea of its graphic interpretation and, as we shall see, influenced the style of the illustrations themselves.

The poet's interest in the illustration of 'The Twelve' and its declamation is evidently explained by a desire to listen to the echo of his poem, to see it not simply translated into different material, but manifested in different forms of art, in order to clarify for himself the meaning of this poem 'written in harmony with the elements.'

Blok himself conceived the idea of an illustrated edition of the poem. Even before its first newspaper appearance he began looking for an artist for a separate edition. His original desire to have the well-known painter and master of the *grande style*, Petrov-Vodkin, as illustrator of 'The Twelve' was not fulfilled, although the latter consented to design the cover. But the very idea of an artist of this kind suggests that Blok saw the visual text of the poem in symbolical and monumental forms.

The first edition of the poem, printed together with 'The Scythians', was a modest one in the form of a brochure. But with it interest in the poem did not abate. On the contrary, it grew. And Blok readily supported the idea of an illustrated edition by Alconost.

II

Legend has it that Blok himself chose Yuri Annenkov as the illustrator of 'The Twelve'. Yet he hardly knew the artist before Alyansky suggested him, although Annenkov was already known by that time, primarily as a stage designer who worked, *inter alia*, in the Crooked Mirror Theatre in St Petersburg with Nikolai Yevreinov, the theoretician of the conventional 'Theatre of the Self'. He also worked as an artist for *Satyricon*, a satirical journal, and as an illustrator of Mikhail Kuzmin's stories. As well as in Russia, Annenkov had studied art in Paris under Felix Vallotton and had exhibited at the Salon des Independants. An aware artist, he was interested in the latest artistic trends, from Expressionism to Cubo-Futurism.

There was a biographical element in the choice of Annenkov. He was friendly with the publisher of Alconost and designed its first trademark. But most important was the fact that for Annenkov, as for the whole of his generation, Blok's name was sacred. After the poet's death he was to write: 'My early student days were full to the brim with his work. I know of no other poet who could have gripped our hearts and minds as forcefully as Blok.

'Our youth grew up under the sign of Blok . . .

'I did the drawings for 'The Twelve' without having exchanged a single word with Blok, fearing our meeting and heeding only the words of the poem.'[1]

---

[1]   The newspaper *Zhizn' iskusstva* (Life of Art), Petrograd, 16-21 August, 1921.

And so it was. The poet's diaries of that period contain fleeting references to Annenkov's drawings, from which we can reconstruct the course of the work on them. Here are a few:

12 *August, 1918*
'Vassiliev and Alyansky came round this evening. Annenkov's drawings for "The Twelve".[2] Komissarzhevsky planning to put on *King in the Square* with sets by Annenkov.'[3]
19 *August, 1918*
'Alyansky came round this evening (Annenkov's new drawing for "The Twelve" . . .)'
30 *August, 1918*
'Alyansky coming round (3 drawings by Annenkov, a new trademark and a poster "The Twelve".)'
31 *August, 1918*
'R. Ivanov leaving for Moscow. Perhaps Alyansky also, so that Annenkov hands over Christ, the old woman and Katya with Vanka.'
3 *September, 1918*
'Evening — Vassiliev and Alyansky with Annenkov's new Christ.'
28 *October, 1918*
'Alyansky (final proofs of "The Twelve" and cover by Radlov N.E.)'[4]
30 *October, 1918*
'Alyansky this evening with the last drawings for "The Twelve".'
8 *November, 1918*
'Alyansky brought "The Twelve" — No. 46 of 300 copies.'[5]
7 *December, 1918*
'Alyansky coming this evening. News from Moscow. Copy of "The Twelve" painted.'

While these notes document the history of the edition, testifying to the poet's close participation in it and indicating the duration of the work and the number of different versions, Blok's letter to the artist written on 12 August, 1918, just after he had received the first drawings, not only throws light on the nature of his remarks, but is of broader significance as the author's commentary on his poem. Like Gogol, Blok also made such commentaries on sug-

---

[2] On the same day Blok wrote the letter to Annenkov about the drawing for 'The Twelve', see section III below.
[3] A play by Blok. The production did not take place, but Annenkov produced a number of sketches for it.
[4] The artist N. E. Radlov was responsible for the type composition and the title page.
[5] The first edition consisted of 300 numbered copies. 25 copies were painted by Annenkov.

gested production of his plays. He evidently attached no less importance to the illustration of the poem.

'Inspired and embarrassed,' the artist recalls, 'I first crossed the threshold of the apartment in Ofitserskaya only after my work was completed and I was summoned to a meeting by a marvellous letter from Blok himself . . .'[6]

III

12 August, 1918 (St Petersburg)

Dear Yuri Pavlovich,

I shall be as brief and business-like as possible, because Samuil Mironovich[7] is waiting and will send you this letter tomorrow.

I was terribly afraid of the drawings for 'The Twelve' and even afraid of talking to you. Now, after looking at them, I must tell you that some angles, parts and artistic ideas are inexpressibly near and dear to me, and the whole is more than acceptable, i.e., I simply was not expecting anything like it, hardly knowing you.

For me personally the most indisputable are dead Katya (large drawing) and the dog (separately — small drawing). These two give me great artistic pleasure and I think that if we, so different and of different generations, were to talk together now, we would be able to say a great deal to each other without spelling it out. Unfortunately I am compelled to write, which is far less convincing.

I am compelled to write for this reason: the more acceptable they are as a whole to me and the more precious the individual parts, the more firmly I must disagree with two things, namely: 1) Katya separately (with the cigarette), and 2) Christ.

1) 'Katya' is a splendid drawing in itself, the least original in general and, I think, the most 'unlike you'. It is not Katya at all. Katya is a healthy, fat-faced, passionate, snub-nosed Russian lass; fresh, simple and kind — swears like a trooper, weeps over novels and kisses with abandon. None of this is out of keeping with the refinement of the central part of your large drawing (the two bent fingers and the surroundings). It is also good that her cross has fallen out (on the large drawing, too). Her mouth is fresh, 'lots of teeth', sensual (it is old in the small drawing). The 'esprit' is coarser and more absurd (leave out the

---

[6] *Zhizn' iskusstva* (Life of Art), 16-21 August, 1921. Later, in his memoirs (Y. Annenkov, *A Diary of My Meetings*, Vol. 1, New York, 1966, p.68) the artist recalled his first meeting with Blok as follows: 'Having finished the twenty drawings, I arrived in St Petersburg with them. There I immediately made Blok's acquaintance . . . Blok said that the illustrations were not really illustrations at all, but a "parallel graphic text, a drawn twin . . ." And again about enlarging the drawings for "The Twelve" to poster size. But how? What for? Why?'

[7] S. M. Alyansky.

butterfly, perhaps). The 'fat-facedness' is very important (healthy and clean, even to the point of childishness). Better leave out the cigarette (she may not smoke). To my mind your small drawing has an unexpected and unpleasant touch of 'satyriconism' not found anywhere else (and quite foreign to you).

2) About Christ. He is not a bit like that: small, hunched, like a dog from the back, carrying the flag carefully and walking off. 'Christ with the flag' is 'both what it says and not what it says'. Do you know (all my life I have felt like this) that when a flag is beating in the wind (rain, or snow, and particularly on a dark night), you imagine someone huge under it, related to it in some way (not holding or carrying it, but somehow — I can't put it into words). That is the most difficult thing, it can only be found, but I can't put it into words, just as perhaps I could not in 'The Twelve' either. But essentially I do not take it back, in spite of all the criticism.

If thick snow were driving from the upper left-hand corner of 'Katya's murder' with Christ through it that would be an exhaustive cover. I can put it like that too.

Now for something else. In Petruka with a knife, the kitchen knife in his hand is good, but his mouth is too old as well. I looked at the whole again and suddenly remembered — Dührer's Christ! (i.e., something totally unrelated to this, an extraneous recollection).

Finally, the last point. I should be terribly sorry if the drawings were reduced. Could not some, on the contrary, be made larger and the whole book published on the scale of 'Katya's Murder', which, to my mind, is such *grande style* that it could be enlarged even to poster size and would lose nothing. Reducing and enlarging are for you to decide.

Those, I think, are the main points of 'criticism'. I could write another ten pages or so, but time does not permit. I press your hand warmly.

Alexander Blok[8]

IV

The artist was not inclined or able to comply with everything that Alexander Blok suggested in his letter. The figure of Christ was not successful although, as we know from the poet's diaries, the work continued on it almost up to publication ('Annenkov's new Christ'). The 'extraneous recollection', as Blok called the analogy with Dührer's Christ in his letter, remained extraneous.

But other figures in the poem received different treatment. This applies primarily to Katya. 'Yes, I took away the cigarette and found a new Katya . . . I met her in a Moscow tavern and drew her from life . . . Yes, I found a new Christ, too, or, rather, removed Christ completely and replaced him by a

8   A. Blok, *Collected Works* in eight volumes, Moscow — Leningrad, 1963, Vol. 8, pp. 513-515 [in Russian].

transparent, formless silhouette merged with the flag.'[9] Comparing one of the surviving versions of 'Katya' with the final one that appeared in the book, we can see that it has been firmly reinterpreted in the spirit of the poet's wishes. The caustic, grotesque figure reminiscent of Toulouse-Lautrec's women has given way to a 'healthy', 'fat-faced', but 'simple' and 'kind' Russian lass, as the poet wanted. And this common female type — perhaps the finest drawing of the poem — not only concretised one of its main figures, continuing the succession of women in Blok's poetry, from the Beautiful Lady to the Unknown Woman, but also personified the simple, folklore structure of the poem's text.

Not only this figure or the figures of Petruka and the Bourgeois, depicted close up, are portrait-like (Annenkov actually included them in his book *Portraits* together with portraits of his contemporaries) but also other drawings of the poem. The revolutionary street with flickering lamps and flags fluttering in the wind, the bullet-pierced windows of the houses and the crooked street signs. All these and other details washed up by the wave of revolution bear the stamp of their time. Their historical authenticity is most convincing. In this sense, too, the drawings concretise and place the poem within the categories of the historical or, as Blok would say, of calendar time and space.

There is in the drawings a second, symbolical level. It is felt in their very style, the sharp, tense rhythm, the contrasts of lines and dots, the endless shifts and intersections which make up their fabric. The very first two lines of the poem: 'Black night. White snow.' are a kind of tuning-fork, a poetic image of Annenkov's black and white drawings. Whereas the artist saw the poem 'as a fresh painting of the newly emergent revolution', his drawings provided a kind of graphic collage of the poem. As a result the representation acquires new meanings: man and his shadow, the object as attribute, the silhouette of the figures as a motif of the procession. Even the most everyday details acquire a symbolic meaning, and the symbols are perceived on the same level as the real details.

Even the Alconost trademark exists here in the same context as the drawings for 'The Twelve'. The publishing house, which began its activity with the publication of Blok's works, was intentionally or unintentionally named after one of the favourite images of his early lyrical poetry, the mythical bird of the alconost (halcyon). This bird goes back to the Greek myth of Alcyone, whose singing was so beautiful that it made people forget everything. Whereas in the first version of the trademark designed by Annenkov, one could still discern the conventional form of the mythical bird, in the new one, specially designed for the publication of 'The Twelve', it appears as something between a

---

[9]   Y. Annenkov, *A Diary of My Meetings,* Vol. 1, pp. 67-68. The artist's list of works (Y. Annenkov, *Portraits,* Petrograd, 1922, p. 146 [in Russian]) contains three versions of the drawing of 'Christ', one of the 'Old Women' and five of 'Katya'. K. Chukovsky recalls that there were as many as twelve versions of 'Katya' (K. Chukovsky, *Chukokkala* (The manuscript almanach of Kornei Chukovsky), Moscow, 1979, p. 33 [in Russian]).

ИЗДАТЕЛЬСТВО „АЛКОНОСТЪ"

demonic figure and the tragic mask of Pierrot or Harlequin, the heroes of
Blok's symbolical theatre drawn from Italian commedia dell'arte. (These
figures were also part of Annenkov's constant set of theatrical and graphic
images, and two years after 'The Twelve' on the cover of Nikolai Yevreinov's
book *The Main Thing* [in Russian] the artist portrayed a crucified Harlequin.)
The sign of the alconost became so closely associated with Blok's name that it
appeared not only on the edition of 'The Twelve', but also on posters for his
poetry recitals as a kind of curtain to the graphic interpretation of the poem and
an iconographical sign of the poet's literary name. This version of the trademark took root in Alconost publications and after 'The Twelve' the works of
Andrei Bely, Alexei Remizov and Vyacheslav Ivanov were published under it,
right up to the final editions of the *Dreamers' Notes Almanack* dedicated to
Blok's memory.

But to return to Annenkov's drawings. They strike a major chord in the book
because of their scale, too. Let us recall that already in the sketches Blok
discerned the possibility of enlarging them to poster size. ('I should be terribly
sorry if the drawings were reduced. Could not some, on the contrary, be made
larger . . .') The book was, in fact, published with a large format and the
drawings acquired a monumental flavour.

The illustrated edition of 'The Twelve' planted a visual image of the poem in
the minds of contemporaries and led to new interpretations of it. An interesting
attempt to project them was made shortly after publication of 'The Twelve'. In
January 1919, in Moscow, Annenkov's drawings painted by the artist were
projected onto a large screen. The showing was accompanied by a reading of
the poem by the actor A.P. Ktorov, with whom Annenkov had specially
rehearsed earlier, acting here as a producer. This fact became known to Blok,
who noted it in his diaries.

It is possible that the illustrated edition of the poem led Mayakovsky to suggest in 1920 that 'The Twelve' be put on the stage as 'a play of an exclusively revolutionary nature'. It definitely influenced Annenkov's work on the mass revolutionary spectacles in which he acted both as designer and producer. It also had a strong influence on the style of the revolutionary poster and on book and magazine illustration.

It can be said that Blok's poem marked the beginning of Russian revolutionary graphic art. After Annenkov, 'The Twelve' was illustrated in Paris by Michael Larionov and Natalia Goncharova, in Berlin by Vassily Masiutin, and in Russia itself by the young engraver Andrei Goncharov, a pupil of Favorsky's, and by the future Constructivist, Telingater, a follower of El Lissitsky.

But Yuri Annenkov was the first.

*   *   *

Such is the brief history of this unique book, the drawings of which on a reduced scale are reproduced in the present English edition of the poem.

To this it must be added that Annenkov was among those who buried the poet in August 1921 in Petrograd, when he produced his memorial drawing 'A portrait of A. Blok in his coffin'. He spoke of the part played by the poet in his life and the life of his generation, the work on 'The Twelve', and his meetings with Blok 'with a pain such as I have never experienced before' both immediately after the poet's death and many years later when writing his memoirs.

In 1924 Annenkov settled in Paris. He worked as a graphic artist, portrait painter, stage designer and cinema artist. His works were displayed at many exhibitions, alongside those of other Russian masters: Chagall, Larionov, Goncharova. The well-known art critics Pierre Courthion and Waldemar George wrote about him. But no matter what else he did, the drawings for 'The Twelve' are the first thing that one associates with his name.

YURI PAVLOVICH ANNENKOV (1889-1974)

Born in 1889 in Petropavlovsk in Kamchatka in the family of the exiled revolutionary P.S. Annenkov.

In 1907 entered the Law Faculty of St Petersburg University and studied art in the studio of S.M. Zeidenberg (together with Marc Chagall), then under Professor I.F. Tsionglinsky of the St Petersburg Academy of Arts (1909-1910).

From 1911 to 1913 lived in France, took painting lessons from Maurice Denis and Felix Vallotton in Paris, sketched in the Laboratory of Experimental Zoology and in 1913 exhibited in Paris in the Salon des Independants (pictures close to Cubism).

On his return to Russia in 1913 began contributing to the illustrated journals *Satyricon, Teatr i iskusstvo* (Theatre and Art), *Solntse Rossii* (Sun of Russia), *Lukomorye* (The Sea Creek), and *Argus*.

Worked as a designer in Petrograd theatres: the Crooked Mirror, the Model Hermitage Theatre, Comedians' Stopping-Place, the Free Comedy, and many others.

Afterword

Took part in the exhibitions 'Monuments of the Russian Theatre' (Petrograd, 1915), 'World of Art' (Petrograd, 1922), 'Society of Easel-Painters' (Moscow, 1925) and many others.

In 1918 produced a series of illustrations for Alexander Blok's poem 'The Twelve' (Petrograd, Alconost Press, 1918, republished in 1923 in Paris: Alexandre Blok, *Les Douze*. Dessins de J. Annenkoff. A Paris, au Sans Pareil, 1923).

In 1920 took part in the staging of the mystery *Hymn of the Liberation of Labour* on the square in front of the Stock Exchange in Petrograd and the mass spectacle *The Storming of the Winter Palace* in Palace Square in Petrograd.

In 1921 produced a cycle of drawings entitled 'Silhouettes of the Paris Commune'.

Published a series of articles on the theatre in various Moscow and Petrograd periodicals: *Zhizn' iskusstva* (The Life of Art), 1921, *Dom iskusstv* (The House of the Arts), 1921, No. 2, *The Arena*, 1924, *The Theatre Weekly*, 1924, and others.

In 1919-1921 executed portraits of Anna Akhmatova, Alexander Benois, Maxim Gorky, Mikhail Kuzmin, Kornei Chukovsky, Boris Pasternak, Alexei Remizov, H.G. Wells, and many others.

In 1924 settled in Paris. Worked as a portrait painter, stage designer, cinema artist and illustrator. Continued to illustrate the books of Russian writers (Dostoyevsky, Nekrassov). Took part in many art exhibitions, including exhibitions of Russian art of the early years of the revolution.

Died in Paris in 1974.

In 1980-1981 Yuri Annenkov's illustrations of 'The Twelve' were displayed at the Paris-Moscow exhibition and at the Alexander Blok Birth Centenary Exhibition (Moscow, Literary Museum).

Bibliography

Yuri Annenkov, *Portraits*. Text of Yevgeny Zamyatin, Mikhail Kuzmin, Mikhail Babenchikov, Petrograd, 1922.

M. Babenchikov, 'Annenkov — graphic artist and drawer', *Pechat' i revoliutsiya* (Press and Revolution), Moscow, 1925, No. 4 [in Russian].

Yuri Annenkov, *Seventeen Portraits*, Moscow — Leningrad, 1926. Foreword by A.V. Lunacharsky.

P. Courthion, *Georges Annenkow*, Paris, 1930.

Yuri Annenkov, *A Diary of My Meetings*, Vols 1, 2, Hommage a Georges Annenkow par Waldemar George. New York, 1966 (Chapter: 'Alexander Blok', Vol. 1).

A. Alyansky, *Meetings with Alexander Blok*, Moscow, 1969 (Chapter 'Publication of the poem "The Twelve" with illustrations').

Alexander Blok, *The Twelve*. Drawings by Y. Annenkov, facsimile edition. Article by L.K. Dolgopolov. Moscow, 1980 [in Russian].